My First Phonics Book

Please go to YouTube and search for the free video that was designed to be used along with this book to teach your child their phonic letter sounds.

The YouTube link information is as follows: [Learn your phonics with learn with Malia – YouTube](#) (learningreasources@hotmail.com)

Or search (learnwithmalia) The 8:51 minutes version.

For the best result watch the video daily with your child and read the book along with watching the video.
Your child will quickly recognise that what is in the video is also in their book. They will also recognise that books are meant to be read by using letters sounds.

It will not be long before they learn their phonic sound and will be racing on to reading. Enjoy the process!

I can say my phonics Sounds.

A...A...A...A

2.

A is for apple.

A IS FOR

I can say my phonics Sounds.

B...B...B...B

4.

B is for bat.

B IS FOR

I can say my phonics Sounds.

C...C...C...C

C is for cat.

IS FOR

I can say my phonics Sounds.

D...D...D...D

8.

D is for dog.

9.

I can say my phonics Sounds.

E...E...E...E

10.

E is for elephant.

E IS FOR

11.

I can say my phonics Sounds.

F..F..F..F

12.

F is for fish.

F IS FOR

I can say my phonics Sounds.

G..G..G..G

14.

G is for Girl.

G IS FOR

15.

I can say my phonics Sounds.

H..H..H..H

H is for Hand.

IS FOR

I can say my phonics Sounds.

I...I...I...I

I is for Igloo.

IS FOR

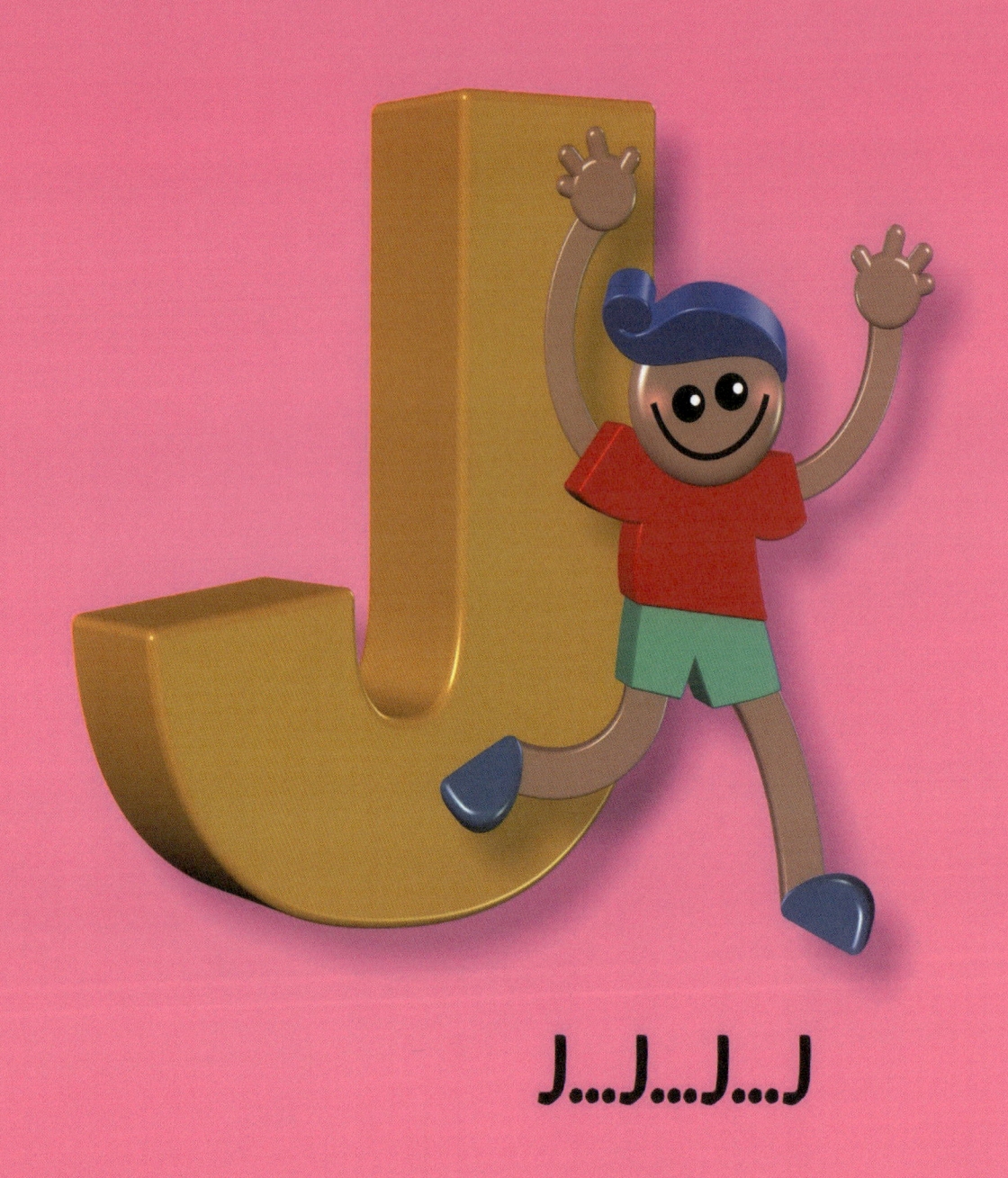

I can say my phonics Sounds.

J...J...J...J

J is for juice.

IS FOR

I can say my phonics Sounds.

K..K..K..K

22.

K is for kangaroo.

I can say my phonics Sounds.

L...L...L...L

L is for Lion.

I can say my phonics Sounds.

M...M...M...M

M is for monkey.

I can say my phonics Sounds.

N...N...N..N

28.

N is for Newt.

IS FOR

29.

I can say my phonics Sounds.

o...o...o...o

O is for octopus.

IS FOR

I can say my phonics Sounds.

P...P...P...P

32.

P is for penguin.

IS FOR

I can say my phonics Sounds.

Q...Q...Q...Q

Q is for Queen.

Q IS FOR

I can say my phonics Sounds.

R...R...R...R

36.

R is for rat.

IS FOR

I can say my phonics Sounds.

S...S...S...S

38.

S is for Sun.

IS FOR

I can say my phonics Sounds.

T...T...T...T

40.

T is for tractor.

T IS FOR

I can say my phonics Sounds.

U...U...U...U

42.

U is for umbrella.

IS FOR

43.

I can say my phonics Sounds.

V...V...V...V

44.

V is for vet.

IS FOR

45.

I can say my phonics Sounds.

W...W...W...W

46.

W is for water.

IS FOR

47.

I can say my phonics Sounds.

48.

x....x....x....x

X is for X-ray.

X IS FOR

49.

I can say my phonics Sounds.

Y...Y...Y...Y

50.

Y is for.

IS FOR

I can say my phonics Sounds.

z...z...z...z

52.

Z is for Zebra.

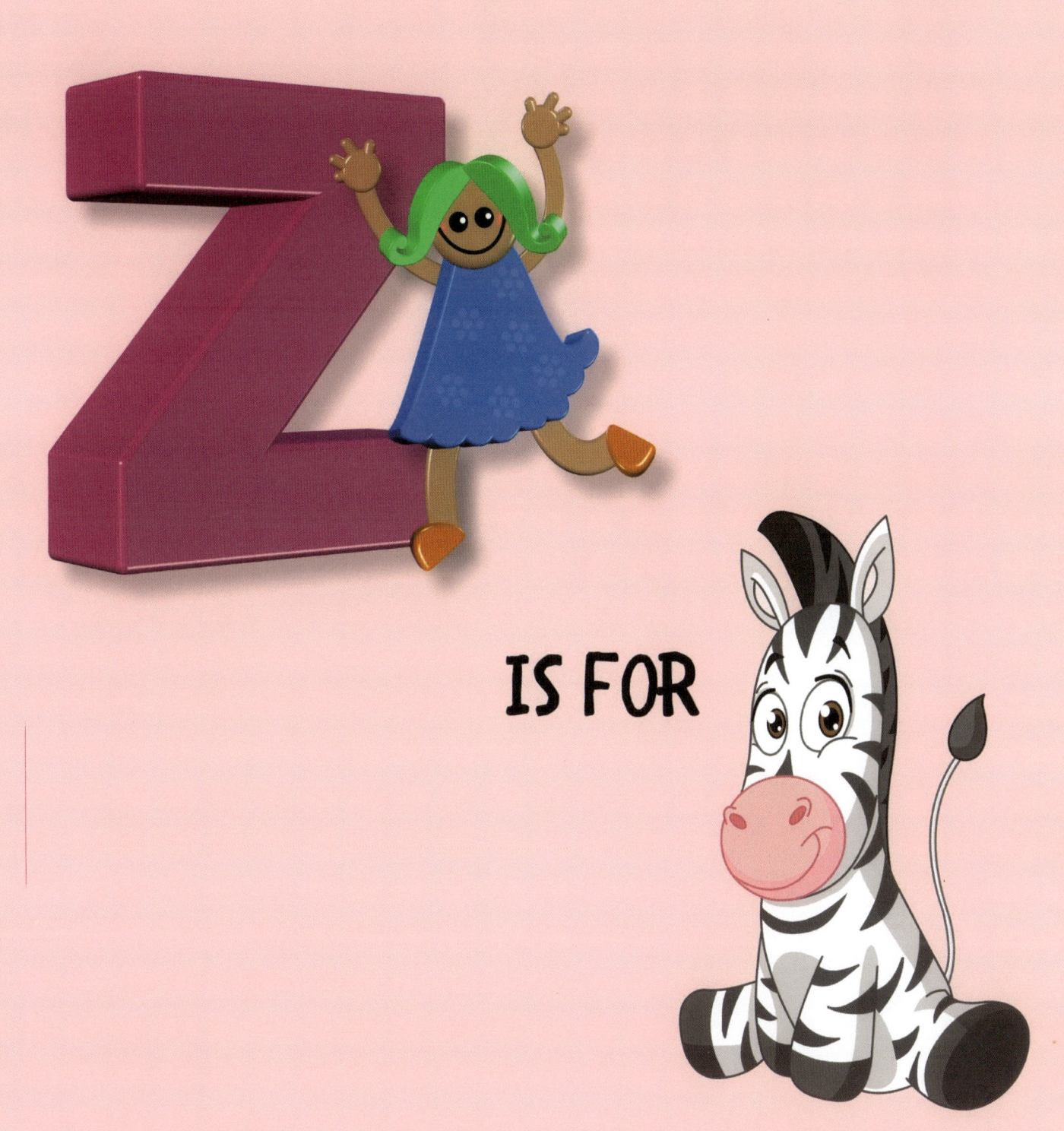

IS FOR

53.

This is a phonics and picture storybook it is filled with lovable animals and characters. Designed to teach the various phonics sounds of the alphabet.
It was developed alongside a free phonic video available on YouTube to assist with the learning process.

(The video link is as follow: Learn your phonics with learn with Malia – YouTube (please use the short version 8:51 minutes)

Research found that It is a good idea to read to babies as early as in the belly. This is a common recommendation to pregnant parent. It is stated that reading to or playing video or music during pregnancy will stimulate vital neurotransmitters in the baby's brain.
The child will be familiar with what was played during pregnancy when they are born. It is also said that it can promote early literacy skills and language development. It can also be a calming techniques to use for a child after birth, if this video and book is use in this way it can make the process of phonies teaching and learning easier for you and your child.

The phonics sounds were done by 3 years & 3- months old Malia, to ensure a soothing child- friendly voice for children.

Authored by Shelly-Ann Espute
Nickela Farquharson &
Malia Anderson

learningreasources@hotmail.com
(More books coming soon)

Printed in Great Britain
by Amazon